RETRIBUTION BINARY

RETRIBUTION BINARY

Ruth Baumann

Black Lawrence Press

Black
Lawrence
Press

www.blacklawrence.com

Executive Editor: Diane Goettel
Chapbook Editor: Kit Frick
Book and cover design: Amy Freels
Cover art: *Chantilly Hush* by Christan Mitchell. Used with permission.

Copyright © 2017 Ruth Baumann
ISBN: 978-1-62557-969-0

Published 2017 by Black Lawrence Press.
Printed in the United States.

For myself at fifteen; for everyone who's been lost like that

Contents

GIRL

A body must reach an equilibrium regardless of its passions toward splintering.

Continue.

Imagine survival as a kind of farming.

Continue.

Are you sure?

THRASH [a study in wreckage]

I.

The sun a spasm. Delirious with too much perspective. The girl moves forward. Sweat of course. Forward subjective of course. *Engulfed: verb:* state of being, state of impossibility. She's thinking of what she misses except she can't think. One thought crosses another like a car t-boning the future. Nesting dolls omnipotent. Gravel sticks to her toes, pinpricks little as a god memory. Something nags. *Here is a body put yourself in it & stay there & stay there & stay.*

THRASH [a study in wreckage]

II.

    After a while the girl turns. To herself but outwardly. At her hands. Are these runaway hands? Runaway bones? A white bird overhead, *no* she instructs *no associations to surrender.* Visualizing a network of escape routes, hollow roads. A skeleton spread across the flatlands. Can it dance? What steps? Nothing but. She sighs. Onward. Like a whistle that brings the dark.

THRASH [a study in wreckage]

III.

    On the road a wildflower. Purple as poison. Remember a vase on a table. Flowers in it. Nothing cracked, no morning light poured on red-edged pieces. Shatter a taught command. What is carved is not followed. Daylight daylight daylight. Her wrists movement factories. Memory unmanufactured. No bottle matters. Brightness like a bruise. A bottle though. How typical. *Go* she does *go further.* The narrative here known. Except for its thumbprint. She holds a lighter to her fingertips. Hail Mary to the temporary. Full of pain.

They say a delayed reaction to an alarming stimulus is a symptom of the body always in emergency mode.

She's weaving a basket.

Inside she'll place something borrowed something breathing something eating.

THRASH [a study in wreckage]

IV.

Hands laid on the body lay still in the body. Ghost leeches parasites of rotten wanting. Ecosystem of the underworld. Closing her eyes a desolate landscape. This for comfort. Imagine an expanse mud-gray. Paled & drought-shrunk cacti like gravestones. In her head she skips. This is where she cannot be hurt. Nothing foreign drags her from herself. No hunt no hunt no sides. It has been a long time. So time no longer matters. Head up now she walks.

THRASH [a study in wreckage]

V.

Motion a waltz bereft of fear. No, saturated & bereft. She walks like an acoustic solo. Without instrument. Just wind. The mind of wind. Dreaming of not dreaming of the night the sky broke. Its hands robotic, grasping. A human cleaned like a mealbone. Once she was picked. In some cultures in some circles of hell, an honor. She wishes now on a full moon. Plucks the hours from her life like petals, terrified there may be no stem.

THRASH [a study in wreckage]

VI.

Wishbones in the head a vortex. Clouds gathered at the nape. Storm a cheap medium. Dissolution, call it progress. Her sleep a glass wall against. Her body collected against an underpass. Rain watches. Keeps score, makes it up. When his eyes were big they were so. Glassy want-mongers million-tongued stupid pseudo-beast. Give a man dominoes & he will fish forever. She shivers. The gutting wasn't so bad. As was the living gutted. Emptiness the loudest papercut. But energy does not die. The raw blankness it feasts.

Do you want to keep going?

Do you feel guilty for having the choice?

Red rover red rover
send hell on over.

THRASH [a study in wreckage]

VII.

Cart pulled to market creates the market. Dirt accumulating now, days tallied. A toenail breaks off like a mile-marker. Destination thirst. Shadow long, shadow needy. Within her mouth many screams no mechanism. A car slows she does not. Supplies a game liquor plays with the flesh. *Curse*? Certain fires have an odor. Is she even visible. *When did you first know?* A hawk overhead. Circling nothing, starving itself. *If everyone dies who wins?* Death scholar. Maybe she's still pretty.

THRASH [a study in wreckage]

VIII.

If a web is cognizant. The poor spiders, all fucked. *Justification: nounverb: uninhabitable sphere.* The girl is not available. A lightbulb flickers in a passing truck. Fog today, like walking into a meditation of last breaths. Tornadoes shrunken & poised, in her for her. Give her this power. Destruction so wide though. A plane becomes a continent. The morphology of chaos. A hand emerging from quicksand her own she steps on it.

THRASH [a study in wreckage]

IX.

Aftermath: one plus a hundred minuses equals. There are turnarounds. The girl doesn't. Red in the sky like crying baby skin. Pluck veins like a harp. Some sound. *Earthly pursuits* she thinks. Furious as a top spinning around itself, its own sun. All planets demoted. Sailors pirates scoundrels delight. Sunset spawning, plummet plummet. When she unrolls dough. When she leaves by her side a rolling pin transformer. No stars just a cough in the fabric. The universe nodding, a shark bobbing in the swimming pool. *If you can't swim, kill.*

THRASH [a study in wreckage]

X.

A snail on the back of a switchblade. Sing a song of disconnect.
Devastation a reclaiming. One way of the world fear. A fence burgundy.
How it impales landscape. Faster now, flight feet on. Sweet morphine
of sleep, its feathers spread wide. A glance is enough. Asterisk *not*. Risk
factor *a bow & arrow in outer space*. Risk factor *how cold the planets*. The
girl asks for a little place to lay her head. She will keep walking after.

SCAVENGER

he wants

to tell you something

under a bridge

in your mouth

behind the pretty part

of your eyes

the dumb part

where you let

BLANK FACED MAN [a study in absence]

I.

Fascinated with the oblique

Aerosol head Blue head

Feet that believe in [redacted]

Feet that move toward [redacted]

He [redacted redacted]

Nothing escapes the flies

They see it all They get it

But he meant to come back

Not to anybody or anyplace Just

BLANK FACED MAN [a study in absence]

II.

Ancestrally who cares

When hands clap they expect a result

A sound An affirmation A value judgment

He digs a little hole Sticks an old self in it

But hollow   Is not   A cure

Have you asked?

A rake hunts the yard. First.

Then the approach of fire.

BLANK FACED MAN [a study in absence]

III.

Illness in light too A power in

Feet are not arrows Except inward Blah

blah Whole life from memory No—

Today he In a catbird's mouth

answers It chews It cries

BLANK FACED MAN [a study in absence]

IV.

Late morning light a hammer

An icebox A shotgun

He does not rise His need does

Load an arrow Never shoot

A birdcall A hollow

This is how one chases With

so little effort *Sludge* he mutters *Bring*

me sludge A paper plane swims by

Rain is a goal Is a throne

BLANK FACED MAN [a study in absence]

V.

Grimy hands grimy eyes

The mice eat stale cheese

The mice eat the mice

Between the toes no Beautification

No Idealization Just spaces

One serenade then One

lullaby then He doesn't set

anybody's table

Above the frame bells toll.

All blood out of

focus. Can you hear?

BLANK FACED MAN [a study in absence]

VI.

If the body is a crime Hell

His lips solemn His head whole

Her age is an appetite Wine on the ceiling

Which is good He'll send her

He'll send her to the ceiling Say a decade

BLANK FACED MAN [a study in absence]

VII.

But impossible improbable Impenetrable blame

A feast laid out For a blind tasteless eater

Yes/no Yes/no   Cesura

in delivery   In deliverance

Masks have a calling They open

a planet to a universe A light

turns on in a basement Pull the string

It turns brighter No/ no No /no

BLANK FACED MAN [a study in absence]

VIII.

After months After bottles shine

their broken light like new faces

After the crowd After the fault lines

lick their sleeping bodies Doesn't

a junky curl into a comma

No sentence Madness origami

Universe situated in a fireplace

O no promise O no hymn

Long walk home So stay

Long night home Do you know

where your handler is?

BLANK FACED MAN [a study in wreckage]

IX.

Hologram Hologram   Have a field day

Burn the blunt The spoon The repetition

of a single song all afternoon Burn the brain

into a hook   Cups catching the rain

Pour them back to the sky   Burn

trust in any mystics   His hand lulls

across dead grass   The earth is stacked so thick

BLANK FACED MAN [a study in wreckage]

X.

Stars pooling like blood No milk

in the whiskey Because the world

is carrion A vehicle A predictable

He will stuff his throat with cherries

It's not hate It's smaller than that

Nobody get a broom Not on

his anti-watch

With thanks

to Tara Mae Mulroy, Jen Charles, Kaveh Akbar, Sharon Hartman, Jimmy Kimbrell, David Kirby, Dorothy Chan, Paige Blair, Paige Lewis, Julia & Autumn for all of their continual support (some writerly, some otherwise).

Ruth Baumann is a PhD student at Florida State University & holds an MFA from the University of Memphis. She is also a co-editor of *Nightjar Review*. Her first chapbook, *I'll Love You Forever & Other Temporary Valentines*, won the Salt Hill Dead Lake Chapbook Contest in 2014. Her second chapbook, *wildcold*, won the Slash Pines Chapbook Contest in 2015. Poems are published in *Colorado Review, Sonora Review, Sycamore Review, The Journal, Third Coast* & others listed at www.ruthbaumann.com.